Scatter Matrix

Books by Abigail Child

From Solids
Climate/Plus
A Motive for Mayhem
Flesh
Mob

Scatter Matrix

Abigail Child

ROOF BOOKS
NEW YORK

ISBN: 0-937804-63-0
Library of Congress Card Catalog Card No. 96-067240

Book and cover design by Deborah Thomas.
Cover art: Bubble chamber photograph courtesy of Lawrence
Radiation Laboratory, University of California, Berkeley.

Acknowledgements:
Parts of these poems appeared in *Chain, Raddle Moon, Torque* and *Two
Girls Review. Climate/Plus* was originally printed in a limited edition by
Coincidence Press. The author wishes to thank the editors of these
publications for their support.

This book was made possible, in part, by a grant from the New York
State Council on the Arts and the National Endowment for the Arts.

Roof Books
are published by
Segue Foundation
303 East 8th Street
New York, NY 10009

Contents

CLIMATE / PLUS

CLIMATE

for Monica Raymond

As 9 motors are formed
    Forgiven majorities of war
Equivocate a silence
    Then she is off

For a certain center of
    Nine motors framed
Management is a permanent job
    Equivocal silences

Signaling you on
    An uncertainty diagram
A kind of speech to frame
    Impermanence

It's a film on the streets
    The quality of the students was low down
Optical signal to pass
    Someone gets in

Silhouetting concentratedness
    Of the students were
Fulcrum to sculpture
    Voyeur

Acquiring artificial intelligence at will
    Glial cells, this RPM
Dreaming connectedness to close up
    The asexuality of the well-being

Fulcrum to work
    As room is book to straighten
Sounds in succession have weight
    Close up to these exceptions

Pressure sound
    Function gets jammed
To hybridize flesh
    Whose business tone is unacceptable (edits)

Comes up with a certain inside muscle
    Edge
Defection to sustain its exemplification
    Hybridized into a four-sided bicycle

Stain a defect
    This is not a ticket
We call it scientific democracy
    Impeachable commute

While everything limits where my wife works
    And uncontradicted bad god
Is contradictory comment
    (All reaction shots)

Limits her pronoun
    Eponymous plummeting
Everything of the necessity that decides the original
    Snow is a novice

The apple folding out of way when not in use
    Slippage is a property of aim
Names' unit
    Itself a machine of the tool

To keep track with the object we are up to
    Error

A conceit is an accent
    Used for ideological serviceability
A machine unflooding
    While the dogginess of her becomes increasingly awkward

Dogmatism undermining the essence of emotional passion
    "Unintelligent, educated and apologist"
Something that goes forward imperfectly
    Machinations' content

Within the context of what we could get
    Would you like your phantasy phone call now?
Of his big breasts
    Settling equally heavy and imperfectly

A touch for equivalence
    You're misinterpreting my enthusiasm
Not that I think flowers are prettier
    Break off of 'big'

Be specific (like Pacific Ocean)
    A violence controlled for pleasure
This is my latest
    Not always he takes them

The perception of movement is silence
    A non-exclusive pacific discrimination
Which follows how music presumed affabilities
    Push down

Thought
    Overlay possibly pun
Memory ply impedance stack saying
    Darkness is the victim of us

Who were saying go for it
    Bloomy for suck
The error seeming grevious to the max
    A formless rococo

Piecing music's keyed affability rap
    Mutations as good as
Questionable shapes
    An interesting vacuum

Critically inflected to
    Stew the recheck and defy
(In retrospect)
    Concurrent wee serial (shapes)

A listing of letters
    That is not subsequent
Anodyne
    An alliance unparalled

Clients don't like it any better than humans
    Fallout from rounding
Impediment flak
    A 9-billion-dollar celebration massacres that

Verifiable facsimiles of the veritable monies
    The machine wouldn't go automatically
Better that humans
    Dismantle this ikon

An anti-personnel bomb
    Or item on TV
Nature looking worse than it is
    Not automatically

A question of taste
    Archlights over-dramatized (grass)
Nuanced
    Extent undressed

Though obviously ads depend on their ideals
    Of modern times
A question in context
    blows up the lip

Of lip over lip
   Unquestionably stiff
Among pictures' disconcerted involuntaries
   Part of a resistable and recountable history

And so attainable
   A source of interest in
To dispense with the obvious
   Is all well

Is the consideration of language
   Alienated to have accelerated the speed of the ordinary
A background source
   Of the dispersal pitch

Repetition as an expansion in context of recognition
   Consider
No genuine maliciousness of you does not emerge
   Source framed to reflect

Infatuation's critique
   Reason repeats
Until the wrong end of the story pays off
   Ingenuous

Slippage
    Alliterative
In the course of regard
    Subject to an extroverted echo

While powder dawn
    Frontiers
Their famous *hubba hubba*
    World argot

If not
    Decoy
Behatted arm of the word
    Designed to make balls of form

Upon their applicability
    Frontier
Inadequate to the inadequacies of our maneuverability
    Please open the summer

Unilaterally
    Globed and shaped in the form of
A head on a background
    Desires to have

What is previously unimaginable
    The design of a torture house in New Jersey
Shadow slow to disarm
    Inadequate forfeit

They want me to fool them
    And then there's a sentence of Lenin's that says
The revolution will pass through Shanghai and Calcutta
    Proceeding

Sentence (next)
    Introject
Slow corollary to time, acqueous and pulsed
    Unnerve the curfew beside patrol

The trial of the social revolution will be scale
    Attention lit by one's capacity
Matrix
    Paratactic adrenalin

Or pan-American blind mother-fucker
    Fact
Analogue to reason's light
    If not from the person

Which models breeding
    While visionary stint fissures
A break
    Written in microterminal hoists and gradually

The utility of view is space
    Struggles from buildings measure down on us
Monumental
    To presume itself as shadow

Point of objective
    Calling totems class ensemble
Modulating the question itself
    Lose the magnificence of its generality

Towards the moment
    A person sees
He's a terrific kisser
    And evolution in all of them

Not a powerless critique
    Nor good as kill them
Which independence writes in
    Breaks up (over war)

Is bent
  For both sides
Evolves
  In complete belief

Capacity matrix
  Electric fog
Incomplete belief
  Writing proliferates both

Material shapes and alliance aspects
  Social city (actually)
Socially wobbly
  Backing up

Not as a gesture of contempt
  But be because intrinsic need encounters space
Divides
  Were noise

Baroque of use
  Whose observe pleasure
Writing is
  Skewed to meet

Commodity torque
    (Still) clackety cups and
Exquisite exceptions requisite meter shock
    Genre

Dependent on a denotative calculus
    A one of a kind
Rain hitting the pavement
    In reverse

Ballast cops
    Requisite drug fairy
Unpreserved
    Heighten the impasse

A kind of consonant mix
    Upon their applicability
Epingles de fantasy
    The world people modify

And then their apartheid
    conspicuous by its absence
Of the equality
    Crosslinked (so called)

You yours
    Your word
Which comes off writing
    Alive in a riot (ridged)

Reasons an ecstasy that is subject
    And would have these ambiguities
Wrestling ownership loops
    Like the objects of its attention

Are released into sense
    And destroyed
Lets down, steers clear
    The point of the frontier effect

Or times you get docked for ignorance
    Dollies back
And reaches hover
    Late last night, a buzz

Imperial disco pursuit
    Combustible computer bodies
Dreaming loops
    Pronounced impetuosity

Demythologize habit
    The entire comic baby with a face of event
Small lights on bus
    The young heels with

Demote
    Or not at all
To omit it
    Not to say

My pet,
    The world resembles writing
What defies these
    Will shadow

Rhythm making sense
    Tacit durable intrinsic twist
To prove it
    Negatively

Fear
    (Unputdownable)
Shot into space.
    A non-privatized valorization

Of their identity be
    Indirectly
Photo-copy
    Loveliness eats away

Magnanimous slave
    And submission (fleece)
Unquestionably *face*
    Used for ideological serviceability

Lies with the original physical attraction
    Degrades
To think again
    Non-sequitur

Thighs
    Decree deliminated space
Apart
    And then become noise

For immediate release
    Surplus desire
Curve
    In the presumption that orients

Spill rod
    Or not fly for cure of it
Cubes aren't slanted
    Now that's *naturalism*

Forgiven majorities of war
    Fly after a silence
The fact that even one child does this
    Makes me lean towards it

PLUS

The contrast beween the occurs
Parenthesizes time and would propose a
Happiness as remote as
The subjects of riot and loss of life

The concept which apostrophes the reports
Of the faction police
Control
Too typical interviews of inequality

A construction of an alternative
Would amount to constitutive awkwardness
Pluralization aggrandizes the difference
And obscures the source

How are we today?
Avoids the explicit hand command
Fear of it licensed
And interestingly absent

This someone is acquiescent
But that communication is contrasted with the present
"In which love has no alchemy"
So inappropriate for his needs

This initial difficulty
Which is not anonymous or similar
Made us the negative
To turn to its difficulties opposite

So a revealing tension exists
A figure strong incomplete
And unfinished

NECROREALISM

NECROREALISM

On the walls of buildings were proclamations: "What does
the red star signify?" Because he can spin a yarn with such

suspense, such innuendoes. And then there opened up
before me the gates of a universe which I scarcely dare

dream about. Oh, come on. The weather is good to stand in
line. If history is to be creative, to anticipate a possible future

without denying the past, it should, I believe, emphasize
new possibilities by disclosing those hidden episodes of the past

when even if in brief flashes people showed their ability
to resist, to join together, occasionally to win. If the order

is reversed, a different pattern is observed. Being as blunt as I
can. Then deliberately she put out the light in her eyes, but

it was still there on her lips—glimmered against her will
in her faintly susceptible smile. Silently, daring not to breathe.

The official figure was slavish, unabled, a muffled-up man
being crushed. From Monday to Friday, from the beginning

of May to the end of July. Upon his return from Siberian exile (in early 1900) Lenin was forbidden to live in St.

Petersburg, Moscow and all the industrial and university centers of Russia. At first her reading made no progress.

•

An occurrence that is an *accident* versus a *deluge*. To substitute one thing for another. To intoxicate and suggest—the essential method of the fiction film approximates it to a religious influence, and makes it possible after a certain time to keep a man in a permanent state of over-excited unconsciousness. *Full of beauty and convincing realism.* The revolution started

on Sunday, January 9th 1905, with a peaceful march of the workers of Saint Petersburg (more than 140,000 people) to the Winter Palace *(Excursion number 3).* As if listening to the explosions above him. Who made an eruption into her apartment and smothered her with smacking Russian kisses. Eating your past—

a kind of necrorealism. *My own wardrobe isn't large,* Lenin used to say. Her charm was in that particular combination of manly, young man's ways—I would even say her male businesslike air with the extreme lyricalness, maidenliness, girlishness of her features and outlines. There are drawbacks to these optical

amalgamations. *Better to be the hammer than the nail* says Tanya. In 1973, construction of five-story walk-ups, which but ten years earlier had accounted for 82% of all the housing built was discontinued.

•

It is *normal*, by which she means *non-explosive*. We adapt to
'reflect' reality. From the edge of the Moika I turned

into the field of Mars. The unblacked-out windows of the house
on the corner attracted me. There is no prose without past,
present and

future

I
                                        would keep catching the
car
in the act of being recklessly sheathed,
                                                    while the-
land   scape itself went
through a complex system   of motion,
the daytime moon

                                stubbornly

        keeping abreast
        of one's head

                                the distant meadows

                              opening

                    fanwise,

the near trees

                    sweeping   upon invisible swings

toward the track,   a parallel

rail line   all at once

          committing suicide   by anastomosis,

                              a

bank

          of nictitating grass   rising

                                                            rising

                                                            rising

---

1. The Soviet authorities would not even consider recouping
the huge investments in housing through rents, which have
remained at the 1928 level.
2. I was probably incapable of expressing his version of indif-
ference—a monumental tapestry, corrogated and ruined.
3. I visualize her by proxy as she stands in the middle of the
station platform where she has just alighted, and vainly my
envoy offers her an arm she cannot see.
4. Once past these, there were only halls with plywood
partitions and a series of stoves under separate bulbs, one of
which burned in heat, pointing to the second floor and drying
sheets.
5. For many reasons, by the 1760s the baroque style was gradu-
ally ousted by classicism.
6. There is of course no actual connection between the two,
but the repetition is characteristic.

•

With a sudden turnabout of his whole body
(although it is strange to say his
whole body

seeing how very little that whole was and how very much
it was not a body)
directing at me the whole bird of his body.

Now write a dictation (having just done something else).
very lovely, very lonesome.
already walking

The Neva is a comparatively young river, no more than 2500
years old. Even
his skull, with that inexhaustible energy of growth

to call hair,
that was hard
was physically perceptible as the surface of the earth's
sphere.

Which in spring burst forth with abundance, ground carpeted
in white violets,
cuckoo birds crowning birches, ice

on the beaches.
But what am I doing in this dreamland?
Somewhere or other (anywhere)

From somewhere or other, from anywhere
when sometime or other
somehow, some way (or other) (in) any way

we use the present tense in the dependent clause
—even though the meaning clearly
is future

•

Now,

the colored pencils in action.

Now,

Aelita at the foot of the escalator.

Now,

clouds in the sky swim in the vast blue emptiness and meet in so many combats and duels that, if I could only snatch a tiny part to put into books or film, I would not have lived on this earth in vain nor have given annoyance to my superiors.

That twist was only the natural extension of the head, its innate completion and outer limit.

(Supplementary information about the comparative)

The consultants watched over what was "reflected." He is thus compelled to fulfill the duties of a whipper-in, as well as those of conductor, instructor and superintendent.

There's a certain level of frustration blemished by glaring failure.

A queue for nothing.

A cast of stupid lips.

As a child of the symbolist epoch, as the epoch's heroine, what could be more important to her than the color of her eyes? Pulling a flap of the jacket toward me, happy that I've found a wordless diverting occupation.

So much the better my dear.

The newest picture had come on screen reversed.

SCATTER MATRIX

Scatter Matrix

Against rotation
this is not personal
tacitly sexed

are ourselves
when same is rotatable
both have jobs

collaborating years in statist periods
impart rotation to the female member
when same is selection

the day behaves personally
tactically sexed
rather than burning or banking

the boy behind the desk takes orders
to fallen shape of *cul de sac*
behaving without thought of future

on overtime
humor is atonal
employee contravened to wax unbodied
wed irrevocable

•

Respectively
let me drink my bathrobe
beneath hot sock of consonant suckers

skin made structure
technically controlled by
inscribed food items

the perfidy of the cooperatant rod
become the daughter
technically possessed

in normalized sound
the periphery of
orifices

correspond
to the cross-section lug
of the instability of

the automatic dream world
to reproduce conditions
of desire
and not repression

•

"Pounds of trees"
is also slit
symptomatic central

designed to pump sound
telephone connected to an erasure
it can't keep

artifact
intends to vanish
while being mathematically proven

seam ikons
symptomatically interrogating Daddy
and laughable

as the dimensions of definition and escape
reveal themselves
a plenitude
of pop up dialogue

•

Therewith,
adorability functions
more radically open

more radically closed
under the suburban zipper
Hi I'm Ian Alger

it is interpersonal
would work if it were harder
not a diagnosis of the whole rotation

palatal desire
rubbing clean
imploding grammars

while monophonic semitones edge lovelies
in acoustic crimps
either visioned

essentially submarine
of figure
and detachable
"cold panel on the spinal"

•

Tributary of
peninsular faces
backstrapping sun

one flesh
one blind
one spot

however illusory
begin to write
with index line

longitudinally split
knocking rain off leaf
to form multiple tongues

unsynchronized
by pulse
charged flight

outside exchange
its scale expands
obviously
into the orifice

•

Asymptotically
admit to fingerhold
a corresponding movement of

section exegesis
under the body *X'ed*
intelligence responds

to the exception
unincorporated and entirely familiar
slidable through a cooperatant

female member
which indents irrationally
bound together
this is not a sonnet

•

In the detour of this
occurrence,
stopped

what is not said
deletes us
blew up

click off
riots down in roaring spate
a burn, a tarn

raining angles incoherence
so much they interact
and are permeable

over-rehearsed
(own)
our over-rehearsed, streaked in dark

unhemmed sun
inflects ground
what is not said
evolves to describe

•

Bounded by four
gouged in the middle
surrounded by camouflage

it lives out its parent
inset with cloisters
roughly corseted

unlike a colonnade
anthropomorphic
interjecting

to make the former the genera
now proposed
grit

a cumbrous lustre
then weight and hardness
plunged
this scale is shown in adjustment

•

A genetic experiment
on the streets of scenario
berserk fantasy stick

with energy credit
split
circuiting

mechanization sprints
gut exiting due
upfrontness nadir

inferior fertilizer in bulletholes
with which leaves
green bang beneath me

abbreviated vivisection
in all that cheer
seemed baroquely metaphysical
reflex

•

We are impatient for a catharsis
what we get is a cathexis
modesty

bookends
of these apes
reputed

played off again
st modernism
what is consuming it?

or perhaps "no" pivots
in direct reference
to arise

intrinsic and non-breakable
and something is removed
unlike anything

"which takes on the burden
of the excellence of happiness"
just to emphasize
love can be accumulated

●

Utopia perseveres
heading unpoundability
reveries

display season consolation
I'm panted serendipity milieu
can form a lasting

respondent scales
to place them together
in the same super family

multivariant rudder springs
euphonious margins
lunger stung forceps goalie

even in his
without obvious relation
read as comely

means an up slash
impossible lipstick
(room for
the green horn in us)

*

Ganglia circuiting star code logistics
(widely)
have a look see

onto amplifications
within the periphery
now I'm busy

stop messages
separate
(option) (orphan) (domination)

good luck
gravel held it
the reaction of the chair on the man

to be sentenced
having capacity
under foot

will rotate
out of the body
you can't subjugate
all have noncommonsense peculiarities

•

And so safe
in spin control
to deter the message

to be pictorially preinduced
eerie
aberrant

remote
awful pink cigarette
(seriously miscast)

antiphony
lost in tongues, pools, back
on pitch

securing his palm
of the spiral rotating through
orifices

listen! provocatively
that's your spirit
that's your fucking consciousness
there is being because there is happening

•

Scatter matrix
in secure sample bands
gormless in vitrio

growing blunter
is this pressed to you
no accident that

the second modification is a counterpart
myth
the slides of the barrel

a lyrical autonomy
vis a vis
essentially intercoastal silence

laid over the other
we're getting more rehearsal
glued on to sky

of the lovers
bleeding and perhaps
even
the compliments of kissing

•

Equalization gawk
mantis diction
flattened replicate charade

kickoff
triangulated neuralization crisis
one earring

things
uncosy
legend

movement towards many
cutting rectangular
5 by 7s

ibid
ancible
pathos of money
they're not hanging this money

•

And so backward
exploded into her age
but it is not numbers

the sky counts
chaos
to impress you in it

imperfectly
pissed
priority

pillow box
counterbalance
stupid

flipside intensity
slit to form
denuded remains laccolite

not on top of shit
stuck query
all her objects have multiple functions
imperfectly

•

Cycles neuralization ism is
father
and further away

canalization translations
knotted proxies
beating down on television temples

sans clock
cast to
flung entablature

in sitio
and horoscope automaton
seen here as

scentless extension
a visible symmetry
circle smoke in well bomb

visible aspects accuracy
it was a secret
groundmass
obliterating the old message

•

In each of us
impartiality wed
sympathetic revelries

tax credit them
(chewing my eyelids)
with reference to gradations

corporals depend entiole
hands become z
punch holes in the diagram

ditching doses in a mall for Mars
prototypically
crank

singlemind
from take-back space
I took it seriously

temperamentally brand-new
in kinky grip of internationalist interviews
buck eye them
a doable ending

•

All metal and expansible
indirectly
I am a zombie

a kind of thick concentrate and its
accompaniment
imprisoned

under the vein
well, almost entirely
on threaded uppers

they make a machine
professing by depending
an anti-romantic

dissipation
falls in on empty
falls to the bottom

plecta pitchfollower
coincide with pitched midi
an impulse
literally naive

•

Delivered from plunder
like someone else's thank you
where there are no clear distinctions

and depression was not easy
in consequence
I love you I love you

and thoughtfully regard
quirk accounts
within being confined
within being very hot

•

This is a chintzy looking torture chamber
this is a Christian state
each division of scale

predates a torso
lassoing hyperbolized and overlagged
gut bucketeers

blacking out
on big girls' blouse
through the inducer
intermittently attach

•

Between coacting suds
which correspond to America light
curved plates

intermittently tongue
provide contact
under a gang

of theoretical shapes
minimalism is about having a dick
orifice to heart's arbutus

afflutter pumps
in polysyllabic tippy toe
throbbing

practicing
flooding emotion
a heat score in long pants

time globe swollen
in spectrum attention
to open code
coerced in body

•

Let us lever
melba blond
boot it

we are lorfing
pawing evolve culture
oxymoron

to rise on its unboiling
rely on the period of gentrification
we call 'country'

the predicament of ambiguity
splashed with non-writing
being flipside

intensity
reveling leaves
capillary snaps

even a dandelion
with an accent
debouched
relay

•

Not just darker
respondent scales inscribe
I am moved by

the multitudes of your intelligence
chock hold libido
pivotally mounted

and co dependent
scalp
when all other spaces are corporate

undercutting love
and that
makes me unhappy

if not quite formed upon
replicate denial
gargoyle

on benadril
is flipside intensity
each word
a diagonal

•

Until deleted

lowered on bedded surfaces

retrofitting

gapper
witwick
without remission

seasoned, we are dogger
this restricted meaning
being developed from
so be it

●

Stem into four
edge of which is rounded
in voluptuous shadows to its physical ambush

shadow complex
on phantasms
with nobody in charge

and she says I am passive
and she says I am quietly moving
borrowing swollen

along automated messages
from moving mouths circled in a band of
nowhere on the map

out of pocket
a collecting motif for my medal of honor
upended reversibility

dissing haptic fission fits
contrarily, I lied
"turned away their eyes
from each others cost"

•

A deliquescence of desire
made ridiculous in bronze
backing pages

from leg
class from inland lake
sun stun stillness

boating
where a host of rapid names
burnt off cracked adhesive

was that the phoneme
you borrowed?
cue to sucker

block
toward which suture
being placed

found impressions rounded
on outer face
and the attached piston
indexes a color

•

They focus force into fuck
and down is pulled
has a name

is the wrong name
is pulled and pulled again
plug on mistake

pleasure aggregates
streaks
or inconstant

arches
take off
from the hem of her garment

with adjoinment
flung
making room a subdivision

begin to exhume
the declension
"in so many sentences
since when since when"

•

Or might be used
unmerely
as this now on mine

unmines meaning
cubist
topiary

meter
snarks
dissenting conscience

to support sunbeam
sufferance
and permeable

genres
in their breathing life
morphic and
unfashionable

•

Seen here as
peroxide
planarian

vertigo
in each of us
tetraploid

of which only
there is no momentum
and it has no synonym

a focus of unequal
border sprees, Maori
predicate

generously ripped and coupled with
how to care for
an original American
and the mode of occurrence

•

Hurrying on the precession
to frame it in upshot
and application of *exactly*

that some of these large wounded looking objects
relatively soft and very heavy
swayed viscera

cheaper than day rates
routine of its performing
limits

which in the end
can be sex malleable
an interdependence

an indecipherable
in sync accompaniments
bouncing of timer effort

to recapture the erasure
the character as author pushes away the sponge
unvalorized—leave it alone
a conservation law is in effect a law of prohibitions

•

Gaggle beat of backup
overness
mugged telephone upends

yap whelps
walking on my tongue
accurately clocked

polyp corking motor dice
reveling leaves even
debouched
inscribe

•

Shifting sheets of simple words
unrecognized succubus
for a gargoyle self

packing person
myopics
undercutting inadequate x

don't
lets
the hours and performance equal times

equal would close over us
in takeout braille
chinked nocturnology

engulfed in cheery proctologist dinner
revolving vowels suck out
justice

an old dream advantage
(before I knew you)
rotate testicle pesetas
adult themes in duped posing

•

Have you considered the cost?
indies of endurance
dowdy gob

and unpatented fantail
ramblas
under lusting foggy faces

cut together on the nuclear poing
fine till you fixed it
get off the needle

tar power scar
plier damage
in the wrong sense, comrade
index of endurance stars

●

Heart of a bottleneck
in ritual vinyl
inadvertencies

a conundrum trapped
of which you are
sleeveless escapism

via satellite body
close to beeper
fuming

in a national protocol
this is over painting
copy stapled

and client driven
soporifically mobile
Chewed

by femmie geegaws
on high band
Felt an involuntary desire
to stroke it

●

Gala beds
jam static
applied to gabbro

with neural displays
in termination copy laughter
a cellular incubation

not apiary silver
but sodder
stringing targets

asylum
chunks
cracking clambers

of slobbers in pictorial explosions
aping
exchange sucked off, see

so much meaning moving
radically figurative and once in person
obviate prehensile quicksand
gunk

•

Aura babble
detachably secured
from amniotic pressure cooker

a mini moment cap on
gambols
with finger grips

its lower end an engagement
lover groove permitting displacements
in threaded uppers

adjacency butternut
wedge manuscript
undreamt against

unplugged
employed in
combination pompoms

kiting clavicles in parenthesis zozzle
jerky animals
inevitably, fruitskins
subject to bath tub yellow jackets

•

Skip ahead kiddo
open the window
non sequitur

shiatzu
for sensation
as interview

banging pigment
gloaming
in swollen runnels

ricocheting name relief by burning
spate rapscallion
with nobody in charge

or is it?
intent on the line
of plugs

stylized wigs
pump and glo
(no scruff)
only heavyweights have scruff

•

Of office after all
and drug attitudinizers
read like a hip episode of *The Prisoner*

but surrealism
will not move the possibilities
deposit something thicker

demur exchange
dismantling equilibrium
snorkly

symptomatic pluck
teetotaler mach bugger
shelled proxy

topiary mass
recollecting
solcor sky

and television's inelegant and unauthentic
paradise
to go beyond
not just run over time

●

Air at last
light
in the predicament of ambiguous intimacies

what's in it for us?
a union
to tell you

mat it boot it
hit the mute button
because cells get crushed

to rise on its unboiling
that you now know
our neglect or vertigo

that every but any one would
might
a might of how

whose
that move but then
and there
there is not the one that thing that wants

•

Mute
cup
to straighten light

and kiss me on the face
fasten love
that does not stop

in the old fashioned sense
basically pictures
reconciliation unreconciled

description is drama
when frame's intent
I'm still living back in these opinions

alertness in static
loss (less
(unless

's sorting out
too much
more until
"its grace abstracted from you"

•